One-Minute
Easter Stories

One-Minute Easter Stories

Adapted by
Shari Lewis
and
Lan O'Kun

Illustrated by
Pat and Robin DeWitt

Doubleday
NEW YORK   LONDON   TORONTO   SYDNEY   AUCKLAND

To Lan's father and Shari's teacher,
Sid O'Kun, who inspired us both

Published by Doubleday, a division of
Bantam Doubleday Dell Publishing Group, Inc.
666 Fifth Avenue, New York, New York 10103

Doubleday and the portrayal of an anchor
with a dolphin are trademarks of Doubleday,
a division of Bantam Doubleday Dell Publishing Group, Inc.

Library of Congress Cataloging-in-Publication Data
Lewis, Shari.
One-minute Easter stories / adapted by Shari Lewis and Lan O'Kun;
illustrated by Pat and Robin DeWitt.—1st ed.
p. cm.
Summary: Twenty Easter stories designed to be read in a minute or less.
1. Easter—Juvenile fiction. 2. Children's stories. [1. Easter—Fiction. 2. Short stories.]
I. O'Kun, Lan. II. DeWitt, Pat, ill. III. DeWitt, Robin, ill. IV. Title.
PZ5.L60n 1990
[E]—dc20 89-32469 CIP AC

ISBN 0-385-24960-8
Text copyright © 1990 by Shari Lewis
Illustrations copyright © 1990 by Pat and Robin DeWitt
All Rights Reserved
Printed in Italy
First Edition

Adapted by Shari Lewis and Lan O'Kun
Additional research by Suzanne Weisberg Lynn

Contents

Introduction

One of the delights of raising children is the thrill of introducing new concepts—new bits of information to the eager and receptive young mind. Everything and anything that happens offers a fresh opportunity for us to enlighten our favorite youngsters.

The traditional holidays are incredibly rich in fascinating levels to be explored: historical, social, and psychological, as well as religious.

Consider Easter—it's like an onion! Peel away the top layer (the Easter Bunny, burdened with his illogical load of eggs) and you'll find tales of Easters of the recent past (such as the tradition that had queens of England pledging to wash the feet of beggars each Holy Thursday). Beneath these stories lie the events of two thousand years ago and the many beautiful Easter legends relating to the death and rebirth of Christ.

But is *that* the origin of this spring festival? Oh, no! Look further and you come upon the ancient Hebrews, gathered around the Seder table (as Jews do to this very day) to celebrate their good luck at being able to start anew.

Have we fully analyzed our onion? Not yet! For hidden away, under all the layers of the history of Easter, are stories from the dark days of prehistory—tales of how primitive people began it all, as they rejoiced at the arrival of the season of rebirth.

Now, kids really savor their "Why" questions, and we think your family will enjoy this glorious holiday even more if you have some good answers to their queries:

"Why do we roll eggs at Easter?" (They've been doing it on the White House lawn for a hundred years, and at the White House they tell us that the egg rolling is symbolic of the rolling away of the stone from the mouth of Jesus' tomb.)

"Why is it called "Easter"? (Stone Age people yearned for spring.

Winter was frightening. Each day the sun gave less light. But with the return of Spring came the warming sun, and new hope. The word Easter is borrowed from the ancient festival of the sun, called *Eastre*.

"What does all this prehistoric stuff have to do with Easter as a Christian holiday?" (The observation of the Easter holiday as we know it started almost two thousand years ago, when people were much closer to ancient traditions. So it isn't surprising that early Christians saw the rebirth of Christ as another of God's miracles.)

Now, there is no need for you to wait for your *kids* to pose the questions. If you know a great answer, raise the issue yourself. You might ask, "Do you know why the robin has a red breast?" (See page 12.) Or, "Why were all of Christ's disciples with him at the Last Supper?" (See page 22.)

Our hope is that these One-Minute Easter Stories will help you to view this holiday with a fresh eye, and that you will pass our enthusiasm on to your youngsters.

Shari Lewis

The Wise Man

Once, long ago, the Emperor of Rome was the most powerful ruler in the world. His armies had beaten all the other armies they had fought, and so there were many unhappy people who had to do whatever the Emperor of Rome told them to do.

These conquered people had to send much of the money they earned to this ruler whom they did not know (and certainly did not like, for he took all they had, and made them poor), and their sons were forced to join the Roman Army and go to lands far from home, to fight (and perhaps die) for the Emperor of Rome.

In some places, this had gone on for many years and the people had lost hope of ever being happy again—until there came a man, a poor man like themselves. He was a Jewish man, a Rabbi (which is the Hebrew word for "teacher"), and he brought encouragement to the people. He was a wise man—a man who spoke of peace in a time when people had forgotten what peace was.

When the people saw the Emperor's soldiers everywhere and wanted to fight them, the Rabbi taught them to smile at the soldiers. He taught that people could be happy if they refused to be *unhappy*.

He said all the things we remember him saying in just *one year*, and yet his words meant so much that they have been remembered from that day to this.

The teacher's name was Jesus.

The Donkey

A poor farmer near Jerusalem had a small donkey which seemed to be too stupid to do any work. The man could not train the beast to carry anything on its back. He felt that he could not continue to feed a little animal like this, one that could do him no good whatsoever. So at the supper table he told his family that he was going to kill the donkey.

His children, who loved the little creature, begged him to sell it rather than harm it. But the farmer said, "How can I sell an animal that won't work?"

His son suggested, "Father, tie the donkey to a tree on the road to town, and let it be known that whoever wants it may have it for nothing." The next morning, that's what the farmer did.

Soon, two men approached and asked to take the animal. "It will carry nothing," the farmer warned them.

"The Lord has need of it," replied one of the men. The farmer could not imagine what the Lord would want with such a useless donkey, but handed it over.

The men took the animal to Jesus. Now, in Jesus' mind, he had seen that the donkey was in danger, and so he had put the idea of giving the animal away into the mouth of the farmer's son.

Jesus stroked the sweet animal's face, and then mounted it with no trouble.

So it was that on the day we now call Palm Sunday, riding on the back of this tiny donkey, the Son of God led his followers into the city of Jerusalem.

If you look at the back of a little Castilian donkey, you will notice that there is a dark patch of hair that goes the length of its back, and another that crosses its shoulders. Legend has it that the donkey has worn this cross since the day it carried Jesus.

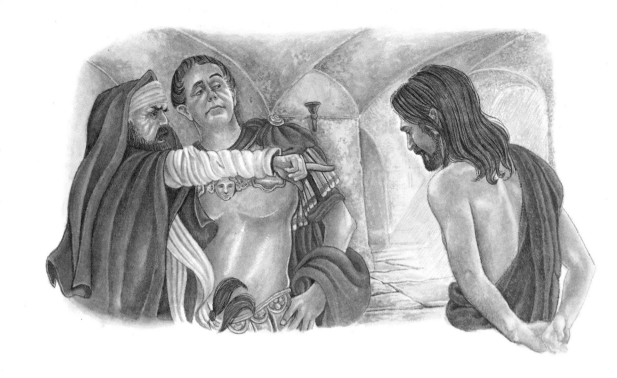

The Robin

Where Jesus spoke, people came to listen. The more he spoke, the greater the crowds. He was thought by some who heard him to be the Savior who, God had promised, would lead the Jewish people to their own land, a land, blessed by the Lord, that would be green enough for their cows to graze, where trees would bear fruit, where flowers would grow, and where the air would be sweet—a land of milk and honey.

Many called Jesus the King of the Jews, and his fame spread all the way to Tiberius, the Emperor of Rome. Tiberius was angered by the idea that there were people who believed Jesus was more important than he.

"King indeed!" he thought. "We'll see."

Tiberius sent a message to his governor, Pontius Pilate, that this "king" should be arrested. So the governor's soldiers found Jesus and brought him to Pontius Pilate, who condemned Jesus to death by crucifixion. They would nail him to a cross. (In those days, that's how common criminals were punished.)

The soldiers stripped Jesus of his clothes, dressed him in a scarlet robe, and put a crown of thorns on his head. Then they laughed and bowed before him.

"Here is our King of the Jews," they mocked.

When they had had enough, they took off his scarlet robe and gave him back his own clothes, leaving only the crown made of thorns upon his head.

The Romans crucified their criminals on the hill called Calvary, just outside the old city of Jerusalem.

They made Jesus carry up this road the very cross to which he would be nailed.

As it is told by some who say they were there, a little robin saw that a thorn from Jesus' crown had pierced his forehead, and he was bleeding. The tiny bird flew down and plucked out the thorn. But as he did, a drop of Jesus' blood fell upon the bird's breast, staining it red.

From that time to this, it is said, robins have had red breasts as a reminder that one of them was kind to Jesus that sad day.

The Sorrow
of the Dogwood

Many years ago, a dogwood tree grew on a hill outside Jerusalem. In those days, the dogwood tree was as tall and mighty as an oak, and this tree was the tallest of all the dogwoods, and extremely proud of its strength.

"Something wonderful is going to happen to me," it said to anyone who would listen. "I'll probably become the mast that holds the big sail on a grand ship, or the main timber supporting a great house."

Unfortunately, the huge old dogwood was cut down to become the cross to which Jesus was nailed. The tree was horrified. All its dreams of glory were smashed, and it groaned in agony as two boards from its trunk were nailed together.

Jesus took pity on the tree, even as he carried it to Calvary. "You will never be put to such use again," he told it. "From this day on, your shape will change, even as will the world. You will become slender and sway easily with the breeze. And instead of acorns,

you will bear white flowers in the shape of a cross, with dark red bloodstains at the side of each petal to show the world how you have suffered. Last of all, the center of your flowers will be marked as though with a crown of thorns, to remind people forevermore that you and I spent our last moments together."

And so it was. And so it is.

On the Way to Calvary

There have been many explanations for the custom of coloring
eggs at Easter. This story is one.

Along the winding road to Calvary, the crowd stood and silently
watched as Jesus, wearing a crown of thorns and carrying the
heavy wooden cross, made his way to the top of the hill, and to his
death. Among those who watched with tears in their eyes was a man
who ran a chicken farm. His name was Simon of Cyrene.

Simon had listened to Jesus' words and seen him create miracles.
He believed that this man whom he now saw suffering was indeed the
Son of God, just as Jesus claimed to be.

Suddenly Jesus stumbled. His cross fell from his back, smashed
against the ground and hurt him. Simon immediately rushed to help.
A soldier tried to stand in his way but Simon paid no attention. He

took hold of the cross and helped Jesus to be more comfortable. Their eyes met for a moment. "Thank you," Jesus said, and Simon suddenly felt as he never had before—as if the sun had risen inside his body.

Jesus caught his breath, and soon was forced to continue up the road. When Simon of Cyrene returned home to his chicken farm, it is said that all his hen's eggs had miraculously been tinted the many colors of the rainbow.

The Fisherman

Jesus had told Peter that he was a king, none other than the Son of God Himself. Peter, a poor fisherman, had watched Jesus make a blind person see. That had convinced him Jesus told the truth.

But now Jesus had died on the cross. He had died, as all mortal men do sooner or later. Peter no longer knew what to think.

Three days later, on the first Easter Sunday, Jesus was alive. Peter saw him. "I do not understand," he said as he looked at Jesus.

"You cannot kill the Son of God," Jesus said. "And they have not. I have risen."

Peter was afraid he was just dreaming. "What do you want me to do?" he asked.

"Go to Galilee and wait for word," Jesus said. Peter did, but after only a short time he told himself that what he thought had happened never *really* happened, and he returned home.

One night thereafter, Peter and other friends of Jesus' went out fishing. They caught nothing through the long night. Then they saw Jesus on the beach. Jesus told them to throw their fishing net on the right side of the boat. They did, and caught so many fish they were not able to pull them into the boat. It was a miracle.

"Feed my lambs," Jesus said. "Feed the hungry. Go into the world and teach that I am truly the Son of the Lord."

Peter wept for joy, and did as he was told.

The Crown

A young prince was once made king and given his father's crown. It was gold, decorated with precious stones, and polished so it positively blazed in the light.

"You must always wear the crown with pride," his mother said, "as your father did. If you can, be as unselfish as he was, and as wise."

"I will try, Mother," he said. And he did. He hired teachers so his people could learn to read. He tried to find out what their problems were so he might solve them. He gave to the poor until he was poor himself.

"I will give away everything, but not my crown," he decided. "For a king must have a crown, and mine is the finest anywhere."

Unfortunately, the boy's reign was short. He became ill and, to everyone's unhappiness, he died. It was the same day Jesus died on the cross. The two met in heaven. Jesus was still wearing the crown of thorns he had been forced to put on that morning.

"Who are you?" asked the young king.

"I am the Son of God," said Jesus, and the boy knew instantly that he was.

"Those thorns are not fitting," the young king said, and immediately the boy gave Jesus his own crown. "A king must have a crown. This was my father's."

Jesus replied, "I know what this crown means to you, and I will wear it proudly, as a sign that I am king not only of Heaven, but of the Earth I love as well."

When Jesus returned from Heaven on Easter Sunday, his head blazed with light, from the crown of the young King.

The Last Supper

It is said that the day before he died, Jesus ate a meal with his friends, called a Seder. It was the first night of the Jewish holiday of Passover, and the rituals performed at this meal are learned by most Jewish children. Jesus learned them too, for he was born a Jew.

Each year, at the Passover suppers around the world, the story of Moses and the Pharaoh is retold:

God sent Moses to Egypt to free the Jewish people. They were being held as slaves by Pharaoh, the ruler of that land.

For ten years, Pharaoh had refused to set the Jews free. To punish the Pharaoh, in each of those years God had made terrible things happen in Egypt. One year, their rivers turned to blood. Another year, frogs overran the land. Then the Lord sent stinging bugs. Moses was afraid Pharaoh would never set the Jewish people free. God was furious Pharaoh had not already set them free.

At last God said to Moses, "Tell the Jewish people that this night I will send the Angel of Death through Egypt to kill the firstborn sons of the Egyptians. Tell the Jews to dip a leafy branch in the blood of a

lamb, and smear the blood on the doorposts of their tents. The Angel of Death will see the mark and pass over their tents."

According to the Bible, on that night Pharaoh's son died, along with all the other firstborn Egyptian sons. But the Jewish children were spared. That did it! Pharaoh begged Moses to lead the Jews out of Egypt.

It is sad to realize that the Passover supper, this ritual of freedom that Jesus celebrated, was the last supper he would eat before he was arrested and lost his own freedom.

The Magic Stone

Once upon a time, long before the first Easter, long before there were cities or towns, when people still lived like animals in caves, they say a man found what he thought was a stone, and brought it home to his family. It was a peculiar stone, not quite round, and very smooth.

Everyone was very pleased with it and stared at it for hours. The children wanted to hold it, but their father would not let them.

And then something very strange happened; the stone *moved*. Everyone saw it tremble. They all stepped back away from it. What sort of stone was this? It shook again. The father reached for his club. He would smash it. He raised the club high over his head, then suddenly a hole appeared in the stone. The hole widened, and the tiny head of a little bird peeked out. Another moment, and the stone split open. There stood the whole bird, which peered at all the people gathered around him.

The man had found an egg, but these early people didn't know that. They thought that life had come from a dead stone. The one thing they *did* know was that they had witnessed a miracle.

The egg has become a part of the Easter celebration. Some say that the little chick emerging from the shell symbolizes Christ's resurrection from the tomb. Possibly so. But surely, whenever we see life appearing where there was no life before—whether it's a blade of grass pushing up through the earth, or a new little bird—we know that we have seen a miracle.

The Greatest Egg

There was once a goldsmith who was the finest worker of gold in the world. He said, "Suggest something you would like to see, and I will surprise you with work unlike anything you have ever seen." His name was Peter Carl Fabergé (pronounced fab-er-ZHAY).

His jewelry was very expensive, but it was magnificent, and all the Kings and Queens of Europe came to him. He had more work than he could handle.

One of the richest rulers in Europe was the Czar of Russia, Alexander the Third. One day, while in Paris, the Czarina Maria happened to look in the window of Fabergé's store.

She gasped, "I have never seen such things. Oh, Alexander, please have Mr. Fabergé make something for me. Please! Please!"

So on the following day, the Czar asked the goldsmith to create some extraordinary golden object for his wife. But Fabergé said, "It will be at least three years before I have the time to make something for you."

No one said that to the Czar! But Alexander replied, "Please" (a word the Czar rarely used), "make something wonderful. I love my wife more than anything."

Fabergé was touched. "What would you like, sir?"

"Anything. But I must have it for Easter. My wife loves Easter."

In 1880, Fabergé made a large Easter egg of white enamel. The egg opened, and inside there was a yolk of pure gold. The yolk opened to show a golden hen with ruby eyes. When lifted, the hen's beak revealed a tiny diamond crown that looked exactly like the crown of Russia—and from that crown hung an even smaller ruby pendant.

The Czar was amazed! Over the years, he ordered a total of fifty-three eggs from Fabergé. Ten cannot be accounted for, but the other forty-three are now in museums and private collections all over the world, and they're worth over four million dollars!

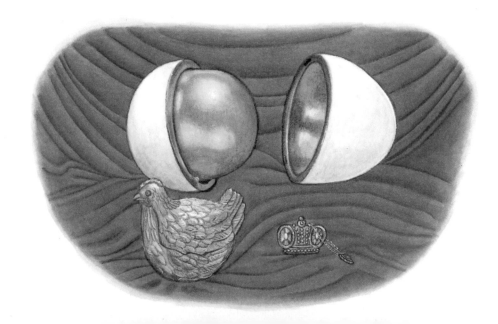

The Foolish Rooster

In a barnyard in Poland lived a rooster whose name was Lek. Lek had magnificent feathers of blue-green, yellow, red, and brown, and a bright red comb on his head, of which he was very proud. Indeed he was proud of *everything* about himself. As he strutted around the courtyard, the other animals secretly laughed at Lek.

There were other roosters in the barnyard, and like them, Lek had many wives and dozens of children. However, Lek thought he was more wonderful than the others, so he was constantly disappointed when *his* children hatched from their eggs as yellow as all the rest of the chicks.

"How can my chicks look like everyone else's chicks," he thought, "when *I* don't look like anyone else?"

Now, at Eastertime in Poland, children gather eggs and paint them beautiful colors, just as we do. That gave Lek what he thought was a brilliant idea.

Plucking out his sharpest feather, he painted designs on a dozen of his wives' eggs. Then he had his wives sit on the painted eggs and he waited.

"My children will not only have magnificent colors," he told everyone, "they will be born with remarkable designs."

Lek strutted before his hen wives, crowing constantly. This so annoyed the farmer that he *sold* Lek. That's why the silly rooster wasn't even there when his children hatched!

Of course the chicks were yellow, as they always are. But Lek never knew, and he made a fool of himself for the rest of his life, crowing each dawn about the gorgeous children he had made one Easter in Poland.

The Horned Beast

It was Easter morning and Rabbit had overslept. The sun was already up, but he had not yet hidden the eggs that everyone would be looking for, under the flowers on the hill. Rabbit was being paid two bushels of clover, and he had not even gone to the hens to *collect* the eggs.

"There goes my clover," Rabbit thought unhappily. He crawled along his little tunnel as quickly as possible, and in a moment popped his head out of his hole. On the grass beside him was the shadow of his long ears.

"My goodness," he gasped. "They've sent a horned beast after me!"

Shaking with fear, Rabbit jumped out of his hole and began running. He ran and ran; around bushes and trees, under fences, and through a stream. But everywhere he went the "horned beast" followed him.

At last, exhausted, Rabbit ducked into a hollow log where, naturally, the sun could not shine on him. There he could no longer see the "horns," and, believing himself safe from the beast that was chasing him, Rabbit promised himself he would never again oversleep on Easter morning!

And he never has!

Fires in the Hills

As their covered wagon creaked and bumped across the great flat Texas prairie, the Deautch family had been seeing the Indians for days. Hans sat by his father's side, held the rifle as his father drove the horses east, and kept his eyes on the distant horizon.

Hans could barely see them, but the Indians always seemed to be there, following the Deautch family. Hans was afraid. The Deautches knew they would have no chance if the strong Indians attacked with their bows and fiery arrows. But the attack never came, and the Deautch wagon arrived at Fredericksburg, Virginia, the evening before Easter.

Fredericksburg was surrounded by low hills, and that first night, the Indians lit campfires on the rim of those hills. A woman from a neighboring cabin brought soup to warm the new arrivals.

"When will the Indians attack?" Hans asked her.

"What Indians?" the woman asked.

"You can see their fires," Hans said, his teeth chattering with fear.

"Indians?" the woman repeated, and she smiled. "No. Tomorrow is Easter. Those fires are made by the Easter rabbits. They're heating kettles of dye in order to color their eggs. Before the sun rises, they'll leave the eggs among the flowers throughout the hills."

Because he *wanted* to, Hans believed the story. But the fact is that every Easter Eve since then, "rabbit fires" have been seen in the hills surrounding the town of Fredericksburg.

The Selfish Giant

There once lived a Giant who had a lovely garden. The children enjoyed playing on the green grass, amid the twelve peach trees and the beautiful star-like flowers. But when the Giant saw that the children were happy there, he changed his mind and sent them away. "My own garden is my own garden," he yelled. He put up a tall wall and a sign that read "TRESPASSERS WILL BE PROSECUTED." He was a very selfish Giant.

Spring came that year as it did every year all over the country. Only in the Giant's garden, it remained winter. Because there were no children, birds didn't care to sing there, and the trees forgot to blossom. The only ones who were pleased were the Snow and the Frost. "Spring has forgotten this garden," they cried, "so we will live here all the year round."

"I cannot understand why spring is so late in coming," muttered the Selfish Giant, as he sat in his window and looked out at the cold. "I hope there will soon be a change in the weather." But for years there never was.

Then one morning when the Selfish Giant was old, he heard birds singing outside his window. It had been so long since one had sung there! He went to the window and what did he see? Children had crept into the garden through a little hole in the wall, and were sitting in the branches of his trees. The trees were so glad, they had covered themselves with blossoms. The Giant's heart melted as he looked. "Now I know why spring has not come here," he said. So he knocked down the tall wall and took down the sign, and from that time on he played with the children all day, every day. They would hide in his beard, and walk over him as he lay down like a mountain, and he would put them in the very tops of his trees—and for ever after, it was spring in the Giant's garden.

A Ridiculous Tale

There are many legends about the town of Gotham, which probably never existed. It was known as the town of fools.

The people of the town of Gotham were known to be ridiculous. In fact anyone who *visited* Gotham was thought to be ridiculous. That's why no one visited Gotham. And because no one visited Gotham the people of Gotham never knew they were ridiculous. In fact they were sure they were wise.

One day the Mayor of Gotham saw a cuckoo bird. He also noticed that it was spring. "By jiminy," he said to his son Richard, "have you noticed that whenever we see a cuckoo bird, it's spring?"

"Yes, Father," Richard said.

"Then why don't we catch that bird and put him in a cage? If we *keep* the bird here in Gotham, we will always have spring." Richard could see the logic in that, and so they captured the cuckoo.

"We will always have spring here in Gotham," the Mayor announced. "My son is keeping a cuckoo bird in a cage." The ridiculous people of Gotham cheered.

Summer came to Gotham, but

it was not a very hot summer, so everyone thought it was still spring, and was happy, except for the cuckoo bird, who became sadder and sadder in his cage. Richard fed the bird until it was so fat it could hardly move—but it grew ever more unhappy.

Richard could not stand the bird's unhappiness, so one day he let it out of the cage and, fat as it was, it managed to fly away. A few days later, fall arrived.

"It's my son's fault," the Mayor announced, and the ridiculous people of Gotham agreed!

The Messiah

(The Most Famous Easter Music)

The great composer George Frederick Handel felt very honored. The King of England had asked him to compose something wonderful to be performed at Covent Garden, which was the King's favorite music hall.

Handel asked His Majesty what sort of music he would prefer, and the King replied, "Why, it will be the Easter season. Set something to verses from the Bible."

So Handel wrote his music. Then the composer rehearsed the orchestra and chorus a great deal. He heard the music many times, and made changes in it right up to the very night on which they would play it for the King.

Handel called what he had written *The Messiah*, which in Hebrew means "He who is an expected deliverer or savior." He named the last part of this powerful work "The Hallelujah Chorus," for it begins "Praise the Lord" and is filled with joy at the resurrection of Christ.

Now, for weeks Handel had been trying to come up with some sort of tremendous *sound* with which to begin this last section, yet he had not been satisfied with anything he had written.

On the night of the first performance of *The Messiah*, as Handel was conducting the opening part he kept telling himself (as he waved his baton) that "The Hallelujah Chorus" was not going to be as wonderful as he had hoped. But when it began, the King was so moved he actually stood up, tears streaming down his cheeks. Well, since *no* Englishman remains seated when his King is standing, *everyone* in the audience got up as well. It created a sensation. The sound of all those people leaping to their feet made such a racket that the added noise gave Handel *just* the sound he was looking for.

From that time to this, whenever there is a performance of *The Messiah*, tradition has it that the moment "The Hallelujah Chorus" begins, the audience jumps to its feet.

Tom Gentry and the Queen

It was the Thursday before Easter, and the Queen's guard was galloping through the streets of London looking for beggars. Queen Elizabeth I was thirty-nine years old, and that very morning she had to wash the feet of thirty-nine beggars. It was the custom for the Queen of England, on Holy Thursday, to wash the feet of as many beggars as her age.

And so it was that Tom Gentry, all of ten years old, was scooped up by a man on horseback and taken to Buckingham Palace. There, before the throne itself, he was told to take off his shoes. Tom hadn't bathed in three months. Nor had the thirty-eight other beggars who had been brought in. These street people had been promised a silver coin when the Queen was finished.

Queen Elizabeth hated this job more than any other, so she said to her lady-in-waiting, "If *you* do it instead, as a reward, you can wear the crown of England all day in your room."

The lady-in-waiting agreed. She wrapped a handkerchief over her face, dressed in the Queen's clothes, and then appeared in the throne room, where she began washing the feet of the beggars.

The Queen hid behind a tapestry and watched. When it was Tom

Gentry's turn, he turned and ran because he was embarrassed at having his Queen wash his dirty feet—and that is how he came to dart behind the tapestry, right where the Queen was hiding. She put her arms around him.

"Don't be embarrassed, little boy," she said. "Your Queen loves you."

She washed his feet, and apologized to the other thirty-eight beggars. She gave them all *two* silver coins to keep her secret, and sent them away. The lady-in-waiting wore the crown all day.

Tom Gentry? He tried to get himself caught by the Queen's guard every year from then on, but never succeeded.

Hot Cross Buns

Once, long ago in England, a monk saw poor families living together in rag tents on the streets of his town. Easter was two days away, and the monk thought to himself, "On the day of the rebirth of our Savior, families should not go hungry."

This monk had once been a baker, so he now baked a great many spiced buns with raisins inside. He decorated the shiny brown tops of the buns with a cross, and while they were still piping hot, he went out among the families and gave them the delicious buns.

A young boy named Giles would not take even one.

"Bake me a basketful of buns that I can sell," he said. "I do not want charity."

The monk looked at the boy's ragged clothes and dirty face, and though he felt sorry for the lad, he saw that Giles had pride, so he baked the child a basket of the buns.

That Easter morning, Giles took his basket from house to house, singing out in a voice that carried over the clear air:

"Hot Cross Buns. Hot Cross Buns.
    One a penny, two a penny, Hot Cross Buns.
    If you have no daughters, give them to your sons.
    Hot Cross Buns, Hot Cross Buns."

Before Mass that morning, Giles had sold all the buns. He put the money he had earned in the poor box at church.

To this day, children all over the world chant the words of his song.

Lobo

In a city called the Vatican, there is a great cathedral named St. Peter's. It is a marvelous place where priests come from all over the world, in order to serve their God.

A very poor man who had nowhere else to live was taken in by one of the most important of these priests, and given a job as gardener. He worked very hard, but living among all those important men, he felt unworthy of this wonderful city. His name was Lobo.

Every day, Lobo left the Vatican with baskets of fruit and bags of bread for the poor. His heart broke to see how many starving people there were.

It was right before Easter, and all the priests were busy preparing for the great day, writing new hymns, composing sermons, and growing Easter lilies. Lobo wondered what *he* could possibly do to thank God for his good fortune.

Suddenly an idea came to him.

Lobo asked permission to use the kitchen. "I want to bake for the poor," he said. For three days he baked. When the priests saw the bread they were very impressed. "Why, it looks like someone with his arms folded, as in prayer," someone said. "But it needs salt."

So Lobo added salt. It was just the thing! And the bread Lobo baked—why, we call it a pretzel!

The King of Butchers

The period of forty days before Easter is called Lent. And in
France, the Tuesday before the start of Lent is known
as Mardi Gras, or Fat Tuesday.

In Paris, it was the custom on the Tuesday before Lent for an ox to
be killed and carried through the streets by all the butchers in the
city, while the crowds cheered. This ox was followed by a cart bearing
the King of Butchers, who was always a little boy.

Once upon a time, the largest ox in Paris belonged to a butcher
named Jabot. The ox, called Peter, was the pet of the butcher's little
son, Alphonse. Every evening, Alphonse would say lovingly to Peter,
"Go to sleep, and know that our Lord is watching out for you." Then
he would place his cheek against Peter's and go to bed himself, right
there in the barn.

This year, a double honor fell upon the butcher Jabot. It was his
great ox that was to be carried in the parade, and so his son was

46

chosen to be King of Butchers. Jabot went to tell his son the news. Horrified, the boy said:

"You cannot kill my ox!"

"But it is an honor to be carried through the streets by all of the butchers of Paris," Jabot said.

"If I am King of Butchers, then *I* make the rules," replied Alphonse.

His father smiled. "A king must have good *reasons* for his rules if he is to be considered a good king." To which Alphonse immediately answered, "The ox is named Peter. Peter was Jesus' friend. Jesus would not hurt his friend."

And that year, with a good deal of trouble, the sixty-three butchers of Paris carried the huge ox *alive* in the parade—bellowing every step of the way, while little Alphonse smiled from his cart and waved to everyone who came to cheer.